My
MOTHER,
Your
MAMA

Stories About Caring for
an Aging Parent

Dr. Ralph E. Plumb & Dr. Feager A. Pertilla

WESTBOW
PRESS®
A DIVISION OF THOMAS NELSON
& ZONDERVAN

WestBow Press books may be ordered through booksellers or by contacting:

WestBow Press
A Division of Thomas Nelson & Zondervan
1663 Liberty Drive
Bloomington, IN 47403
www.westbowpress.com
1 (866) 928-1240

ISBN: 978-1-5127-7626-3 (sc)
ISBN: 978-1-5127-7627-0 (hc)
ISBN: 978-1-5127-7625-6 (e)

Library of Congress Control Number: 2017902578

Print information available on the last page.

WestBow Press rev. date: 02/23/2017

My Mother, Your Mama

Stories about Caring for an Aging Parent

Dr. Ralph E. Plumb and Dr. Feager A. Pertilla

Contents

Foreword

America is aging. Despite the visible presence and rising influence of millennials and gen-X-ers, our population is growing old. The US Census estimates that by 2030 we will have nearly one million people over the age of one hundred. As a practicing doctor specializing in hospice and palliative medicine, the proper care of the aging in today's society is a topic near and dear to my heart.

After bringing 1,110 babies into the world and walking with families during their most intimate health care moments, I am now at a place where I focus on a segment of the population that is often forgotten: those who are aging and who cannot fully care for themselves. Currently, fewer people are able to save or invest enough to meet their financial needs, let alone support themselves in decades of retirement. Beyond the well-worn concerns about finances and health care, especially of the elderly, there are even more poignant and problematic issues: *How will they live? How will this aging population manage to define a meaningful quality of life? Who will be there to assist, nurture, motivate, and provide them with the essentials of day-to-day living?*

This is where Ralph Plumb and Feager Pertilla fill the gap. They bring to life the ups and downs, the joys and sorrows of caring for an aging parent. The music of their diverse voices and cultures blend together into a vibrant song that captures the poignant universal experience of addressing the challenges of caring for aging parents. Though influenced by distinct cultural perspectives, they deal with similar issues. Though managing vastly different psychological and cognitive dynamics in their parents and varied family support systems, their struggle is the same: *How do we make life work for our aging parents?*

I first met Ralph when he served as CEO of International Aid, Inc., a significant nonprofit health and human services organization, where he led two thousand volunteers and employees as an energetic force to improve the quality of life for the poor and disenfranchised around the globe. *My Mother, Your Mama* is a natural and beautiful extension of that vision and work. Together with Feager, a compassionate educator and leader in her own right, they seek to help today's boomer generation improve their quality of life and that of their aging parents.

Journeying through their stories, readers will gain a glimpse into an intimate reality that the majority of us will face. It is not all pretty or warm or sentimental. It is often thankless, inconvenient, awkward, and abjectly uncomfortable. However, this book provides valuable yet hilarious lessons that can guide readers through their own journeys with aging parents. Embracing humor and compassion, Ralph and Feager invite readers into this essential work that we cannot abdicate to social service agencies or the health care system.

The most important thing while on earth is relationships. The relationships we have with our parents, at any stage of life, are formative and significant. I watched my own father suffer from esophageal cancer for six months, before he finally died. He had a bad end-of-life experience. Aging is inevitable—languishing should not be part of the equation. I only wish I'd had *My Mother, Your Mama: Stories about Caring for an Aging Parent* as a companion on the journey to help me make sense of the roller coaster of thoughts and emotions that ran through my mind and heart in those moments.

John Mulder, MD, FAAHPM, CHMD
Chief Medical Consultant for Hospice and
Palliative Care, Holland Home
Medical Director, Trillium Institute

Chapter 1

Transitions

*I*n 2014, when November was federally proclaimed to be National Family Caregivers Month, there were sixty million caregivers, and the number was quickly rising with the escalation of aging Americans. While this statistic is interesting, it never really meant anything to me until I found myself caring full time for my elderly mother. I had always cared for my parents … but from afar. Very far.

After leaving home and finishing college, I married and settled with my family in California while my parents remained in Connecticut. Living on opposite coasts was a two-edged sword. A blessing and a curse. I was far enough away to enjoy my freedom, independence, and professional growth, but I was too far for my daughters to have much opportunity to get to know their grandparents.

Still, I had a regular routine that included making sure my parents had what they needed. I traveled frequently for business and always arranged to fly through Connecticut at least once or twice a year to take care of their home repairs, important paperwork, or finish whatever larger projects they had left undone. Afterward, I would treat them to dinner, stock their fridge with food, and then return home three thousand miles away. This was our regular routine for more than thirty years.

Then suddenly I was tending to them up close, and it got personal. No longer was I the dutiful son living on the West Coast and checking in faithfully every week. I was a "caregiver" 24/7. I knew the time would come. I just didn't realize it would be so emotionally and physically challenging to do all that was required. Being a caregiver began invading my sanity, and I wasn't sure how I would survive.

I am the only child. Simply speaking, there is no one else who can handle the decision-making and responsibilities that naturally fall to me. After my father died, caring full time for my mother was an unwanted surprise, like a nightmare that crept up on me while I was watching.

Over the years, my parents took care of each other. They bought their own food, cooked their own meals, and kept each other company. They were a good match. My mother constantly talked, and my dad slowly lost his hearing. Then the day came.

Eventually, I began to worry that my dad's health was declining and that my mother was running herself ragged driving him to various doctors multiple times per week. As my dad fought issues with his heart, battled diabetes, and struggled to triumph over other maladies, I spoke with them about moving to California. They gladly agreed.

So I undertook the complex task of moving two aging parents across the country. I carefully chose their home in a quiet retirement community, not too far from where I lived. I flew east many times. I tackled sorting, packing, and shipping the last fifty years of their life. I sold their house and extra furniture and filled dumpsters with decades of accumulated paraphernalia.

My parents were pack rats, Depression babies who saved everything in case a tornado hit, a tsunami struck, or the country crumbled into anarchy. I found their stash of security: empty potato chip bags rolled and bound together with rubber bands, stacks of margarine containers, and slivers of soap from the 1980s. I stumbled across paper towels and Styrofoam plates that had been used, washed, and dried for future use. I know I should not have been surprised, but I was.

When I was young, I was embarrassed by the clutter. As a teenager, I rarely invited friends over. When I did, I made them close their eyes on their way to my room, which in contrast was always spotless and organized. I even rigged a pulley system from my bed, so I didn't have to look at their mess and could shut the door without getting up. To this day, I am a neat freak. My house is tidy, my office is well arranged, and my car is pristine both inside and out.

By the time I relocated my parents from Connecticut to California, my dad was walking with two canes. During a layover to change planes in Chicago, it literally took him almost thirty minutes to walk fewer than a hundred feet from the gate to the restroom, do his business, and return to our seats. When we arrived at my parents' new home, it took nearly a whole day to review each light switch, storage space, bathroom amenity, and room location. Then I made a mistake. I bought my mother a car.

"This isn't like the old car," my mother complained.

"It's the exact Toyota Echo you had in Connecticut," I said.

"It's not the same." She crossed her arms.

"It is the same. The same model, year, size—"

"*This car* is bigger."

It didn't matter how much I tried to explain. No sane reason or logic could change her mind. So I dropped it and focused on a far greater quest: getting my mother retested and re-licensed at the California DMV, so she could drive my dad to his many doctor appointments.

Obtaining a California driver's license can be challenging, but securing one for my ornery mother was a feat worthy of knighthood. It all started after a long wait in the lobby, when the clerk called her name.

"Rita Plumb?"

"Mom, they're calling you." I nudged her a little to encourage her to stand. She stayed glued to her chair.

"That's not my name," she insisted.

"Rita? Rita Plumb?" The clerk scanned the crowd.

"It's your name legally—"

"Shush! I told you. That's not my name."

I sighed and rose, approaching the counter. My mission? To convince the clerk to use my mother's middle name only. I grinned. Most people like it when you smile. I was hoping the clerk was like most people.

"Look, my mother hates the name Rita. She does this every time we go to the social security office, to get medical records, at every public agency. Can you please call her Louise? She won't come if you don't."

The clerk just stared at me. I motioned to the amazingly still dark-haired woman sitting erect, fingers primly on her purse, looking everywhere but in our direction.

"You have a mother, don't you?" My eyes pleaded.

The clerk groaned and shrugged. "Louise Plumb?"

As my mother shuffled to the counter, I thanked the clerk who soon forgot and mentioned the dreaded "Rita" again. My mother unleashed a tirade, and I wasn't sure whether to laugh or cry.

My mother needed to take the written test three times on different days before she passed. Finally, she graduated to the eyesight test. I saw another perfectly kind government clerk who was about to have her day ruined. My mother stood before her.

"Okay, ma'am. Cover your left eye and read the fourth line from the top."

My mother wrinkled her nose and shouted, "What? I can't see that! It's too small."

"That's fine, ma'am. Just read the second line."

"Don't be ridiculous! I can't see that."

"No problem. Come over here." The clerk guided my mother to another device. "Place your forehead here and read the third line."

"Are you kidding?" My mother stepped back and looked at the clerk as if she was a Martian. "It's too dark in there! I can't see that. No one can see that."

At this point, I couldn't help but laugh. It was like watching Laurel and Hardy, except this time I didn't have to be Laurel.

Somehow my mother managed to pass the eye exam and progressed to the road skills test. This was also a scene—or so I heard, because I was not allowed in the car. In the car that wasn't *her car* but was really the same as her car, my mother braked to a sudden stop many times and then accelerated like a bat out of fire more than once. By the divine grace of God and our perseverance, the state of California finally granted Louise a license.

This began the ordeal of "patterning," to teach her how to drive the two miles and required two turns to travel between my parents' new home and the doctor. I might as well have been trying to direct my mother to drive to Italy. It was a major effort that required weeks of practice and repetition.

For six months, my mother figured out how to get her husband to all of his doctors without ending up in Mexico. Then dad was hospitalized. It was difficult. It was sad. We waded through our grief. Dad died a few weeks later. And then caring for my mother got hard. Really hard.

You see, my dad wasn't my birth father. He was the kindhearted man who married my mother and adopted me when I was five. Even after my dad passed away peacefully, my mother refused to identify my biological father. For six decades, she kept him illusive.

"It's none of your business," she said whenever I asked.

"How can it not be my business? The man is my natural father." I fumed. "At the very least, I need to know to know my medical history. Fifty percent of my genes are his."

"You have 100 percent of my genes, which has nothing to do with him."

My mother remained as stubborn as a block of ice, consumed by her secret. It gnawed at me as I gradually, then increasingly, and finally unequivocally became the primary caregiver for my widowed mother. She was ninety-two years old. During my time as her caregiver, I moved her into my home, then out, and then back in again. I had moments that ranged from pensive reflection and appreciation to blood-pressure-popping frustration and irritation.

You may have something in common with me and the millions of baby boomers who are riding the emotional roller coaster of caring for an elderly mother. We love our parents, but they can drive us crazy, especially as they age. You may be the only child and feel alone beneath the weighty fullness of care and decisions that fall on your shoulders or you may have brothers and sisters that you can get along with fine at family unions. But when trying to effectively care for an aging parent, it feels like war when it comes to deciding collectively about the house, money, who does what for Mom, and how it gets done.

Within the realm of obligation and responsibility, caring for an aging mother is a complex nexus of genuine intent and frustration, love and pain, affection and sadness. We often wrestle with the range of conflicting emotions. We are motivated by understanding that our mother needs us, so we do everything we can. Yet our own needs scream to get met, like time and attention for our spouse and children, our personal privacy, and our right to an opinion—not to mention our sanity.

I have discovered that it is not necessary for me to deny my frustration or feel guilty about it. However, moving through my shock and anger into a place of acceptance has not happened quickly or the way I expected. It actually started the moment I encountered my friend and coauthor, Feager. That day I realized the key to surviving this journey was not to travel it alone.

The afternoon I met Feager, we were waiting for a local college board of directors to gather. We both served and were a bit more punctual than the rest of the board. But their lateness turned into a sort of salvation for me.

I started to share with Feager the experience of caring for my mother. Well, let's be honest. I complained about it. I discovered that Feager was also in the process of caring for an aging senior. Soon we were chatting, chuckling, and swapping parallel stories. Although our respective moms had vastly different personalities, came from distinct cultures, and fostered diverse family environments, Feager and I shared a commonality. That alone is like medicine for the soul.

As our conversations became more frequent, I discovered Feager has a unique and understanding perspective regarding my area of need as well as the realities and challenges of my individual experiences. Somehow, just talking help. It helps a lot. Eventually, we started sharing our stories with other caregivers of elderly moms, and those people risked revealing their own topsy-turvy journeys along with the rawest of emotions.

So now we share these true stories with you. They offer key moments on our own honest journeys, which are still ongoing, and include the jaw-dropping experiences of others. We hope these tales make you laugh or even cry, if that is what you need at this moment. Feager and I have found that both are necessary in this ministry of compassion involving nurture, care, and advocacy for elderly parents.

As fellow sojourners, we invite you to travel with us. By choice, we have climbed into this gut-wrenching rollercoaster of hilarity and sorrow. There is a reason why roller coasters in amusement parks always have more than one seat. Laughter is best shared with others.

One of my favorite lines from a Clive Cussler novel is, "Only time, failure, and sorrow can make you a wise one." The wisdom of unconditional acceptance is a long journey. It is why Feager and I cling so tightly to God and see His role as so important. Move over, Solomon. I now understand.

God, and just everything in general. Even though Mama is now approaching one hundred, nothing about this has changed. This is because Mama is a planner. She organizes and arranges her entire environment to fit the design in her mind. She takes charge of her own care. Really, she has placed me and my sisters in categories and that's where we stay. Each of us does the specific task Mama has assigned, just like when we were young. Except instead of washing dishes, taking out trash, and raking leaves, we now have "senior care" chores.

I am given the task of making sure Mama is well taken care of. My oldest sister lives with her and tends to her daily needs, and my middle sister takes up the slack. Zenobia chauffeurs Mama to her appointments. I buy the things she needs. Mama has us all trained well. She hasn't cooked in ten years, since the passing of my dad.

Occasionally one of my sisters takes her out to dinner or brings her favorite take-out, but I usually do the cooking and put her meals in containers. I make her fried chicken, black-eyed peas, and cucumber salads. I'll prepare beef tips, rice, with cabbage or collard greens. Sometimes she just speaks her mind: "Spaghetti." So we eat Italian. If Mama wants a steak dinner at Lone Star or the Sizzler, then that's what Mama gets. If it's Friday, then going for fish or shrimp might be on our menu.

On Sundays, one of us drops Mama at church and another picks her up. While all of us are churchgoers and have deep relationships with the Lord, none of us attend the same house of worship. We're so tightly woven that it's surprising this is the one area of life where we break free. Everyone belongs to a different congregation, but I think those at Mama's church love her best. They all call her Mama Coe. She can point to most everybody and say how she trained them up in some way in the Lord. Mama Coe is a pillar for them, a pivotal force. She's a prayer warrior and an encourager. They won't start church without her.

You might think I'm exaggerating, but I'm not. One Sunday morning, my sister was late bringing Mama to service. She's usually very punctual. In other congregations, worship happens whether you're there or not. In Hope Community, worship waits for Mama. I heard that someone suggested starting without her. But the people raised their voices.

"Start without Mama Coe?"

"We need to wait for Mama Coe!"

"No, we won't start until she's in her seat." Yes, Mama Coe has her own seat. She doesn't require it. Mama just sits there all the time. So no one else does, out of respect.

Before and after worship, she holds court. The family of Christ, old members and new, come to greet her, hug her, kiss her soft cheek. She receives them warmly. Blesses them. Lifts them up as only a wise, stately queen can.

This homage isn't the only thing that amazes me about her. While she never held a college degree, Mama has more common sense than anyone I know. I have a PhD in education, so I know a lot of smart people. I've served as a principal and superintendent of schools. I've directed a ministry training institute and have been a board member of the Association of Christian Schools International. Still, she's got one of the quickest minds I've ever seen. She can read a situation and is seldom wrong. She can sense danger and see deeply enough into people to love them unconditionally—even people she doesn't know.

Mama's strength comes from her ability to pray through any trial. She prays daily—Monday through Sunday, name by name, for *everyone*. She prays every single day for people such as Oprah Winfrey, President Barack Obama, the ladies on *The View*, Bob Barker from *The Price Is Right* (even though he retired from the show almost ten years ago), all the various news anchors, her pastor, my pastor, members from her church, my church, your church … well, you get the picture. Call me if you want to be on her list.

When my sisters and I were young, Mama taught us to pray everyday. We all would go with Mama into her bedroom, the "prayer room," and kneel. Dad never joined us, because she prayed too long. Looking at her list above, can you blame him? Mama would get started and then transport to some place in the spirit. She spoke plainly, so we followed right along. Sometimes one of us would doze on our knees. Be careful, if she caught you asleep. Mama wasn't so caught up that she couldn't see. She'd pop you on the arm, pat your behind gently. We'd spring awake, prayerful as ever.

Today my sisters and I are all women of prayer, each in our special way. Mama will call me during the day and say, "Let's pray for …," so I'll stop and join with her in the moment. But I'm not like my older sister, who has a different style. She

Chapter 2

Mama, Precious Warrior Queen

I am the youngest of three sisters. Together we care for our mom, who just turned ninety-three. When Dianne, Zenobia, and I were young, Mama gave us special nicknames. She'd call us Feebee, Little Di, and Little Mama. Sometimes she'd call me Deedee or Wheatie, but Feebee mostly seemed to fit me best.

She was like the mom on that old Kool-Aid TV commercial. She always had great snacks for the neighborhood kids who jumped rope and played hopscotch with us in front of our house. When my dad was overseas for military service, she made sure we were well cared for and protected. She took good care of her three girls. She always knew her limitations and worked around them.

Mama never took no for an answer. She handled her business, our business, the family business. She seemed ready to face anything. Nothing rattled her too much. She was very practical about life, living on this broken earth, is an intercessor like Mama. They can go on for hours. For them, it's as if only fifteen minutes have passed. I'm fervent in prayer but not repetitive. That's more Dianne's style. She's what I call "a prayer lister." Every night she prays with Mama or has the list of who needs what, and she faithfully carries people up to the Lord.

When we were teenagers, Mama did devotions with us, and we had scripture to memorize. She was always teaching and singing to us, "Jesus is on the mainline ... be an overcomer ..." Mama is an overcomer. She's an organized overcomer.

When our dad passed away, we had to make arrangements. My sisters and I just couldn't wrap our brains and arms around doing all the preparation. But Mama, grief-stricken as she was, took control. As we finished one small task, she hastened us to the next and so on. She wouldn't allow us to get stuck at any point. At the end of the ordeal, I suggested we redo the will and have a living trust done. She quickly agreed. I guess she didn't want to have to look at any of this again or think about us having to look at it without her. Mama was a warrior that day—clever, too. She still is.

Mama shows her courage and smarts, even when we go to the doctor. On this one occasion, I had to take her in early to get her annual blood work and other samples done. We were told to be at the lab by 6:30 a.m. For whatever reason, she was very nervous that day. When they called her name, she almost collapsed. I asked what was wrong, but she brushed it aside, saying, "I don't know why I'm so nervous."

Well, I found out. It was because she has what's called rolling veins, which are what nurses and phlebotomists call veins that move around when you try to take a blood draw or insert an IV. Mama's technicians were great, and they used the same kind of needle as they do on babies, so all was well. The whole time, Mama sat without complaining, because she knew it had to be done.

She had to give a urine sample as well. So we both went into the restroom, because I was going to help her as usual. I got the jar for the urine and held out my hand, ready to take her purse. She suddenly said, "Get that brown bag out of my purse for me." I followed her order, of course.

"Look in the bag." I opened it and inside found a tiny jar with the top tightly sealed. "Now take the urine out of that jar and put it into the one for the lab."

"What?" I couldn't believe what was going on. I'd heard of people trying to pass a drug test this way but couldn't imagine what she was doing.

"You heard me. I'm too old to squat and pee. I did my own sample this morning, so we could just transfer it to the lab jar." So logical. So organized. So Mama.

We both began to laugh so hard. Tears streamed down our faces. I can't imagine what it sounded like on the other side of the door, but we didn't care. I always knew she was too smart for her own good. I'm glad Mama landed on the right side of the law because she'd be dangerous on the wrong side. Her plan is always efficient and tight, just like it was the day of the great urine sample.

Now, if you want to get Mama really riled up, go ahead and mess with one of her three girls. No one escapes. Not even us. If she spots anything she doesn't like, she'll say in a second, "You may not have a father anymore, but you have a mom. I can't drive. But I can catch a taxi!" This is her way of letting us know she's still capable of taking care of business, just like when we were young.

We're forever begging her, "Mama, please don't get in a taxi!" My sisters and I follow her instructions. Why? Because we know she's more than capable of hopping into a taxi to go about the business of trying to take care of herself if we don't.

She is convinced that her plan is best. Once she commits, she's in for life, especially when it's *her life*. She knows what she needs, and she gets it—one way or another. So Zenobia, Dianne, and I stay in our categories and work together to overlap when needed. Just like when we were little, it helps us get along. We're glad to do it Mama's way, because … well, she's our precious and smart warrior queen, who fought so hard to give us the life we have.

Chapter 3

Mom's Pedicure and Big Foot

I thank the Boy Scouts for teaching me self-sufficiency. I learned the essence of their motto: "be prepared," and many other valuable life lessons. I even rose to the rank of eagle scout. Despite such useful training, nothing could prepare me for my elderly mother's toenails.

As a man now taking care of my mother by myself, I wasn't fully prepared for the range of challenges I would face with things like personal female hygiene and selection of clothes. Truthfully, I never paid much attention to my mother's feet until one day during a visit to her house she mentioned they were hurting.

"Take off your shoes." I helped her slip them off and then jumped back with shock.

The nails on my mother's feet sprawled over the rim and around her toes. They were taking over her feet, just like those creeping vines that strangle you in a horror movie.

My mother stared at me. Unfazed, waiting for me to say something.

"Put your shoes back on," I said, a little wary.

She obeyed, without spouting opinions or rebuff, which shocked me even more.

"Come on."

"Where are we going?" she asked.

"To a nail salon."

"Which one? Where?"

"Anywhere." In that moment, I had no idea where. But I didn't care. The mission was clear.

We hopped in the car and drove straight to the closest nail salon I could find. A sweet Vietnamese lady guided my mother into a lounger and gently propped her ankles on the footrest. She seemed so nice. I wanted to warn the manicurist but honestly didn't know how I could possibly prepare her for what awaited.

When my mother slipped off her shoes, the poor woman nearly fell off her stool. She looked at me, the feet, and then at me again. Deadpan, as if I had just told a bad joke. "I can do nothing."

Our knight in shining armor ended up being an experienced podiatrist, who seemed willing and amazingly able to work on my mother's toenails. He seemed almost excited at the prospect.

The challenges didn't end there. My mother's toenails were just the beginning. Soon I was washing her sheets and clothes and discovered threadbare intimate apparel. I held up her granny drawers to the light and watched it shine through.

"Mom, we need to buy you more underwear."

Other than admiring bras and panties on a poster walking past a Victoria's Secret store, I never thought much about buying them—even though I was married and have two grown daughters. Yet the bra and panty quest with my mother more resembled black and white newsprint ads from big-box stores in the weekend paper.

Once in the store and safe from the summer heat, I took a deep breath and asked a question I never expected to utter to my mother: "Okay, so what kind of underpants do you wear?"

My mother, ever helpful, widened her legs into a slight squat and in a loud resolute voice said, "The kind that go like this." Her hands motioned around her groin area. I really didn't want to look, but it was either that or let my mother go freestyle—and believe me, no one wanted that.

"Like what?" I inched nearer. From the information provided by her sweeping fingers, she could have been describing diapers.

"Like this. Right about here."

Her awkward clarification only confused me so I decided to search the racks, only to discover a blizzard of options: boy shorts, hipsters, V-line, V-kini, retro-lace, French lace, Brazilian, briefs, biker shorts, thongs. I started to sweat, not wanting to delve deeper into any of this.

I figured underwear ending in "-ini," "lace," or "thong"

was out of the question. Then I got an idea. "Here, Mom. Let me look at the inside label."

She turned, and I flipped over the waistline of her underpants. I scoured the rim along my mother's slowly diminishing frame, but anything resembling a tag was long gone. Exasperated, I motioned to a store clerk stocking shelves. To me this salesperson seemed like an angel, because somehow my mother and I managed to leave the store with six pairs I prayed would be sufficient.

Bras, panties, and pedicures? These are things guys just don't think about. Usually we don't ponder the power of feet unless someone is trying to kick us or we're hunting Big Foot. There are some sons who will do anything for their moms. I must be one of them, because I have hunted "Big Foot" for my mother. No lie. No exaggeration.

During one particular stretch of time, after my father died and after I already had tried living with my mother once, I moved her into a first-floor apartment. It was in a nice multifamily complex with lots of trees and birds. Trees and birds are her favorites. I felt proud for having found such a lovely place. With her furniture and belongings in place, the cable TV working, the wall phone installed, and a fridge full of food, I thought all would be right with her world. I thought we were going to be okay.

Silly me.

If a tree falls in a forest and no one hears it, does it make a sound? For my mother, every noise is an earth-splitting quake that rumbles and signifies the end of the world. All of us have our own level of tolerance for noise. Having traveled to more than a hundred countries and found my way through blaring spots like Mexico City, Beijing, Paris, Cairo, and Mumbai, I have developed a solid gauge for how loud human beings can be.

One of my academic degrees is in interpersonal communication, so I even find the general human tolerance for noise and the ability to adapt to be a fascinating phenomenon. You might think that observing my mother's increasing sensitivity to sound as she ages would perhaps be interesting to me.

However, when it comes to the woman who gave me life, my studious objectivity and scholarly interest fly right out the window. Just when I think I've succeeded in satisfying her, I discover I haven't. When I provide what she says she needs, she is not happy. I love my mother, but she drives me nuts.

Not long after move-in day, my mother called me—whispering, frantic.

"Mom, what is it? What's wrong?" I heard her angry little gasps and flutters through the phone.

"That one upstairs," she said. "It's Big Foot."

"Mom, we met the person upstairs."

"I hear noises."

"It's just the neighbor."

"No! That one upstairs is diabolical."

"She's a middle-aged woman with a cat."

"She is satanic. And they know I know."

My mother and I are Christians, so Satanism is serious

business. The seemingly simple, quiet, single lady living upstairs appeared harmless. But I didn't like the idea that somehow a "they" might be involved. As crazy as my mother makes me, she is still my mom. So I devised a plan.

"I'm coming over," I told her.

"Finally," she said.

"I'm spending the night."

"Good. See you soon, son." She sounded relieved, and I supposed that was sufficient for now.

You might think my mother is lying or manipulating to spend more time with me. While I'm the first person to admit she is a hardcore and thoroughly capable manipulator, I know the difference between raw and feigned fear.

When I arrived, my mother opened the door with a face that was truly grateful.

"I'm here now, Mom. You can go to bed.'

"What are you going to do?" She seemed almost concerned.

"I think I'll stay up a while."

"Good idea. You keep watch." She retired to her bedroom. Eventually, her light went out.

I looked around for a place to spread my work. I had much to do before my next business trip. I spotted the dining table and converted it into a temporary desk. Soon I was brain deep into strategic management models and recommendations for resource acquisition, leadership development, and organizational effectiveness.

"What's that noise!"

I jumped from my chair and floundered my pen over

the edge of the table. "What noise, Mom?" I snapped as a demand. I normally don't startle easily, but in bare feet my mother is a ninja.

I turned to face her. With wide eyes and a white nightgown, she looked like a little ghost. "That noise!"

I strained my ears and heard hot and cold water rushing through pipes, turning on and off, interrupted by the clinking of porcelain.

"Geez, it's the upstairs neighbor. Probably washing dishes." Then I sensed the light creak of an old floorboard.

"What's that?" My mother clutched a shoulder. "Don't you hear it?"

"Yes. She's doing that terrible thing called walking. Probably going to bed, which is where you could be if you really wanted."

I stayed overnight a few more times to make sure my mother was safe. Yet this was all I ever really heard from Big Foot. Still, I stuck with my mother through every innocuous sound she heard.

This eventually subsided, and I'm glad we went through it all if it meant her quality of life was improved.

Then, one day, "they" start calling her on the phone.

"Who are they?" I asked.

"I don't know. But the phone rings at all hours."

With each passing day that I talked with my mother, the stories grew more intense about the errant calls. It sounded bigger than "Big Foot." Something serious. Soon she was telling me they were calling at night and she couldn't sleep. Once she counted the phone ringing thirty-two times.

I wrestled with the best options. I fully believed each phone number received a certain percentage of robo-calls, wrong numbers, and telemarketers. At this point in our history, I lived some forty-five minutes away and couldn't climb into the car every time my mother felt annoyed at the world.

I had her phone number changed and made sure it was unpublished. The respite lasted about a week. Then the tales of terror began again.

"These phone calls are horrible," my mother insisted.

"What do you mean?"

"People don't say anything. There is just breathing and also noise in the background."

By this time, I was starting to hear static in my head from all the nitpicking and complaining. But I just couldn't push from my mind that my mother might have been getting prank calls. Maybe someone was targeting her? The elderly are vulnerable. They are a prime mark for phone scammers and thieves.

"This time I let it ring forty-two times." She sighed, helpless.

So during the next visit, I decided to teach my mother how to unclip the telephone cord from the wall jack. My thinking was to help her develop a routine with the landline, so she could relax, be peaceful—and so both of us could get a decent night's sleep.

"See, Mom. Press here. Unclip. Pull. In the morning, press in the same place. Plug in. Okay, you try."

"Oh, that's a good idea." If it's anything my mother loved, it was a good idea. It was nice to agree on something, to receive her appreciation.

I watched her carefully, feeling a bit zen. She repeated the process many times, but I worried that in the morning she would forget to plug the cord back into the jack.

"I won't forget." She scurried for pen and paper. "I'll just write it down."

I watched her grab a sheet from the side table. *Oh great,* I thought. *Write it down on the same paper where you have scribbled my phone number three times along with the names of your granddaughters, whom you sometimes call Hal.*

But my worries apparently were unfounded. My mother developed a pattern of unplugging and plugging in the cord without any problems. To our mutual relief, she was sleeping at night, and I was flush with pleasure that she was so trainable.

Then, during a particularly busy work week, I missed one day of checking in with my mother. She didn't call, so I dialed her. The phone rang and rang. There was no answer. For the next two days, I called constantly. I heard only more ringing. I was exhausted. I called Feager, who encouraged me to heed my instinct and swim through rush-hour traffic to make sure my mother was still alive.

I arrived close to 8:00 p.m. It was getting dark. The apartment complex was settling in for a quiet night. I knocked on the door more times than necessary. It slowly opened, and there stood my mother, alive and grinning. I caught my breath. I didn't even realize I'd been holding it.

"Hello, Ralph. What a surprise."

"Mom, do you know why I'm here?"

"No, I didn't know who it was."

"No! Mom, do you know *why I'm here*?"

"Well, no …"

"I haven't talked with you in three days. Didn't you notice?" I slid by her, entering the apartment to scope the place for hidden intruders. No overturned chairs or furniture out of place. She didn't fall, knock herself out, and then forget.

My eyes landed on the wall jack. I saw the cord limply hanging, not fully inserted so that the plastic safety had clicked into the socket.

"No, I put it in right," my mother insisted. "It must've fallen out. This phone is crazy. It doesn't work properly."

No, you're not working properly! I held back from shouting this at her. Instead, I just clicked the cable into the wall. My gaze met hers. "Didn't you even wonder a little why no one has called you for three days?"

"No, I haven't heard Big Foot in a while. Everything is fine."

I tried hard to follow her logic but gave up. *Everything is fine?* Everything was fine, except I wanted to bang my head against the wall. Evening birds sang in the trees outside the open window. I caught the soft laughter of children playing and dogs barking as the summer sun set. Maybe this would stop me?

I stared at the crisp taupe of a recent paint job coating the wall. No, I still wanted very much to punch my fist through into the adjoining apartment. But I didn't, because I knew it would be just one more thing I would have to fix for my mother. There was already too much for me to do.

I took a deep breath and remembered that I still needed to phone Feager. In the deepest core of my being, I call on the name of Jesus. I called on Him again and again and again … so glad He is always here to listen.

Chapter 4

Mama versus the Cable Beast

I hate to be interrupted. Today I'm at work in the middle of a strategic planning meeting for an important project. The future educational years of many children are at stake. The project is time sensitive, and there are ten people working alongside me. Together we're developing, organizing, and undertaking multiple assignments to implement key curriculum and programs for the benefit of teachers and students. It all falls on my shoulders to lead this quality team to get everything done, on time and with success.

I've got my groove. I'm totally focused. I'm flying high with possibilities. Then the phone rings. I pick it up. On the other end is Mama in full panic. I can hear it in her voice. My heart skips a beat and then starts to race.

"Feager," she says breathily. "Feager, I need your help!"

By this time my heart is galloping out of control. Mama is home by herself. Something is wrong. Really, really wrong. I'm trying to think, but every split second brings a new terrifying thought. *What am I going to do? Mom is an hour away. Both of my sisters are at work. They are equally as far.*

Then I feel Mama's frightful anxiety. This woman who remained calm in the face of my dad's death, who can demand obedience with the slightest glance, who has walked every difficult road in life with poise and her head held high, this strong, determined lady is doing something I've never seen. She is panicking and using my full first name.

I am paralyzed. I can't speak. My lungs are shallow. My mouth is dry. In this moment, I don't even have the sense to look for a glass of water, even though I'm standing right next to the water cooler. *Is it a heart attack? Is it a stroke? Is someone breaking into the house? Did she fall? Is she okay? Oh my goodness, is she okay?* The office suddenly grows very big and then shrinks, practically strangling me. I unbutton the top clasp on my suit. I struggle to breathe.

"Feager, the TV won't come on!" she says.

*The TV ... oh my goodness, the TV ... I knew it, something terrible ... what can I do? Now I'll have to—*I stop. *"What did you say, Mom?"*

"I can't get the TV on. Please, tell me what to do."

"Mom, you almost gave me a heart attack!" I sink into a nearby chair and exhale, calming what could be my oncoming stroke. I look at the conference room and see ten worried faces peering at me through the glass. My team knows I care for Mama. They see how important she is in my life. They worry for me, because I worry for her. All work has stopped.

"I'm sorry, baby." And I know she is. I can hear that in her voice too. "I need you to go through the steps with me again."

I nod and wave my workers back to their task. "Sure, Mama. First, you have to find the remote. Do you have the remote?"

I launch into the steps. She follows along, and the TV comes on. She's happy, but I have a headache that's as huge as the United States. I take a deep breath and try to stuff serene thoughts into my mind, "Mom, in the future, could you please ... *please* ... not act like the world is coming to an end when you call me when it's just the TV?"

"Okay," she says. I hear her smiling to smooth things over from the other end of the line. "I'm sorry. Thanks for your help. I love you."

Now what do you do with that? She loves me. I love her. All is right with the world.

This scenario has happened more than once, more than twice, more than three times ... and I could go on. As an educator, I expect my students and those I supervise to learn, so I do the same. Now, before I panic, I make sure that Mama is not calling with an emergency—well, an emergency as I see it. However, I have to keep reminding myself that for her, a dead TV is an emergency.

I've realized that for Mama, and many older folks like her, TV is like a friend. It's her company in a quiet house that is lonely and without conversation. It's a voice that reaches out to her the entire day, until my sister gets home or until I stop by or happen to call her on the phone.

Don't get me wrong. Although she is ninety-three years old, Mama isn't some fragile daisy. When that television turns off and refuses to turn on again, Mama is going to figure out how to get it back on.

There have been times I haven't been available to walk her through the steps. So what does she do? She hops on the phone and calls the cable company. She has done it so much they know her by name. Literally, *by name*. I'm surprised they're not all addressing her as "Mama Coe," like everyone at church.

One time she called and the cable guy came by to see what was wrong with the TV. She couldn't turn it on, and I couldn't seem to walk her through getting it on. When she phoned the company, a technician came out right away.

"There's something wrong with the cable," she says.

"You're right, there is." In less than a minute, he detected the problem and leaned down to fix it.

"I knew it." Mama's natural state is this kind of confidence.

"You didn't plug in your TV." The technician attached the cable, turned on the television, shook his head, and exited.

I try hard not to giggle when she tells me this story. We've all been there at some point, with some electrical cord—the toaster, the computer, a cell phone, a clock,

The next time she called, someone rushed out to the house again. She told the new guy, "There's something wrong with the cable.'

"For the cable to work, the remote needs to work. Your remote isn't working."

"Well, it should." That's Mama, always quick to tell it like it is.

"I imagine it was. Until you de-programmed it."

"I was trying to fix it."

"You touched all the wrong buttons."

"I told you. I was trying to fix it. Something was wrong with the cable."

The technician sighed, reprogrammed the remote, and left her with this helpful advice: "Lady, here's a tip. When something is wrong with the cable, it's usually not the cable. It's the cable user." After that, I'm pretty sure she was praying for his soul as he walked back to his truck.

Some scenario like this happened at least four more times. Every time she called, the cable company came and made an adjustment to resolve the problem.

One evening while I was visiting Mama, the TV went down. This time I called the cable company. I dialed, waited for someone to answer, and then politely reported our dilemma. When the operator looked up Mama's file on the computer, I heard him stifle a laugh.

"We've had a technician go out there several times already."

"Yes. And?" I didn't like his tone.

"Well, it's been for ... let's just say ... minor problems."

I heard between the lines. This guy was intimating that Mama was nuts. Now, if she really was crazy, I probably wouldn't have minded the comment. But she's not and deserved some respect in her time of need. My eyes widened. My voice got crisp. My lips pressed together hard.

"Look, she's not nuts. You're dealing with a senior, and the TV is important."

"Sure, lady. Whatever you say. We'll be right out. Again."

I hung up calmly but wanted to punch the guy. I didn't, because I am a "lady" and Mama's daughter, and we all know she raised me better than that.

The technician arrived. He checked the television cable, but it was firmly plugged in. He fiddled with the remote and found it healthy as a horse. Mama and I watched him "ahem" and "aah" and "uh" for quite a while.

"Something is wrong with the cable," he said.

"Really?" I couldn't help smirking at him.

"The problem is on our end."

"Really." I narrowed my eyes at him.

He tinkered for a bit and then called the company. I think the operator may have felt a little stupid when he found out.

"Yes," I wanted to say. "Sometimes that aging senior who has lived three times as long as the rest of us really is seeing something with her failing eyes that we can't see. Sometimes, there really is something wrong with the TV. How many times have you accidentally left something unplugged? Haven't you ever forgotten to turn on your alarm more than once and arrived late to work in the morning? Misplaced your keys? Left the lights on in your car?" Yet no one attributes these blunders to age. When a middle-aged adult does these things, they're just "mistakes." People giggle, say oops, and move on.

The cable beast isn't the only alien Mama has had to battle. On another occasion, her clothes dryer stopped and wouldn't come on. My oldest sister was there with her working on the problem but just couldn't get the machine to function. Mama called me, convinced that she had the best solution.

"It's old, Feager. We need a new one."

"Okay, I'm on it." We ordered the dryer online. But it took hours to decide which one might serve her best.

The new dryer finally arrived, but it didn't solve anything. The machine wouldn't work. Mama had a great hookup, but now she needed a different kind to accommodate the updated technology. This meant finding an electrician. We all stared at the bright black cable. There it was, ready to be the big answer to Mama's wet clothes dilemma. As I dialed for an electrician to fix this problem, Mama just kept staring down that cable.

"Let's just get the old one fixed," she said suddenly.

"No, Mama. That's not a good idea. It'll probably cost as much to fix this old one as it will to buy a new one." I pointed to the shiny machine just inches away. "The new dryer is already here." *Who wouldn't want a brand new dryer?* I had to focus on holding my tongue. For me, the answer was clear.

But Mama had her mind made up. And when Mama has her mind made up, no one except God is going to change it. My sisters and I know this, so we don't bother arguing with her anymore. She figures out what she wants and goes for it, one way or another. Since Mama was usually right, my sisters and I just did what she thought was best. It was her washer and dryer, right?

We called a repairman to come out and fix the old clunker because Mama didn't want to be bothered with having her electrical sockets fooled with.

Do you know what the technician did to fix Mama's massive problem? He *plugged the cord* into the wall socket. That was the major step. To help for the future, he also put a new control panel on the dryer so she could see the cycles. The machine came on. It now works whenever she needs it. She's happy. Overall, I suppose that's what counts.

Sometimes it feels as if I'm living in a parallel universe. There's the work me and the mom me, except the person I'm caring for isn't a child. The work me supervises projects, creates curricula, teaches and trains personnel, implements district-wide programs, and always has her feet firmly planted on the ground. I'm a grown-up and glad to be one.

Then there's the mom me, who springs into action whenever there's trouble. I leave a meeting of ten people to leap to an old woman's aid, no matter what the mission. I fly to the phone. I speed dial to save the TV. When she calls, I drop everything to make sure she is okay.

But I remember how this tiny, soft-hearted woman with an iron will always stood ready to save me, especially when I was a child. She kept me from danger, bandaged my boo-boos, and gave me wings so I could soar through life and be such a strong support for others. This is why I suppose I don't mind zooming between universes at lightning speed or conquering beastie things like naughty cables and grumpy technological devices that don't cooperate.

Most people don't believe in superheroes anymore. But my Mom does. Just ask her. I think she sees heroes every day and prays for them in her time of need. She is probably very much like the other six million elderly over eighty-five struggling for respect in our country today.

Chapter 5

Always Talking

My mother has diarrhea mouth. This might seem like a harsh thing to say about the woman who labored tirelessly to feed and clothe me for eighteen years. But if there is anything my mother can appreciate, it is an honest, no-nonsense assessment of a person.

I came to this conclusion after a thirty-year personal study. The observation began slowly and then dawned on me as I continually watched how my mother acted. She brings new meaning to the words spitfire.

Words give my mother courage to be anything she wants. If what comes out of her mouth didn't make me cringe so much, I just might find her fascinating. For my mother, words are a defense against what she dislikes and desires to keep at a far distance. It's a full-time job, given my mother's lifelong disdain for so many things—especially doctors. It doesn't matter how nice they might be, how much they want to help her, or how extensive their knowledge. I think this adamant resistance stems from a single misdiagnosis of tuberculosis when she was a teenager back in 1938. To this day, my mother pitches a fit when it's time to go to the doctor or get a blood draw.

"You mean they're going to stick me? With that huge needle? *In my arm?*" At this point, she usually glares at me—betrayed by her only begotten son. "What for? Why should they do this?"

"Mom, the doctor says—"

"I don't need a doctor! I'm not sick!" When my mother ramps up like this, her Connecticut accent grows thicker.

And so most every conversation goes regarding semiannual check-ups, monthly follow-ups, and any other appointment in between with someone who wears a white lab coat. I think my mother believes if she can just keep up her constant string of questions, preferably ones that require lengthy answers, she can prevent the inevitable.

But there is no preventing old age and the eventual breakdown of our bodies, just like there is no stemming the torrent of hot words that flow from my mother. Since many researchers hold the belief that women talk more than men, it might be easy to chalk up my mother's jabbering nature to the vast number of twenty thousand words women use daily.

However, in our family situation, I think the phenomenon started happening when my dad began to lose his hearing. Very early on I got used to the pattern of having my mother repeat everything someone said or was spoken on TV, even when my dad was not in the room. Whether my mother started doing this because my dad couldn't hear well or he developed not listening as a defense against her, I'm really not sure.

"There's a slight chance of showers," the weatherman would report.

"It's going to rain tomorrow," my mother echoed.

"Yes, Mom. I heard. I'm sitting right here."

"The president just held a press conference and said—"

"I know, Mom. The economy is slowly recovering. We can expect a dip in the unemployment rate."

"Did you hear that?"

No, I can't! I can't hear this. Please, not again! In these moments, especially during the years she is living with me, I focus on the plop-plop, fizz-fizz of the antacid I'm getting ready to gulp in order to stay sane and ulcer-free. It's necessary just to keep myself from exploding all over her.

While parroting reporters is a big part of daily life, the most poignant reason my mother has always talked so much, the root of why nearly every fleeting moment has been filled with words, is that she became accustomed to not having anyone to carry on a conversation with her. My mother could keep up a steady stream of communication into the air, expecting only once in a while to get a grunt from my dad—or if she was lucky, a couple of spoken sentences.

When I moved away to college, I adapted my dad's technique and took it one step further. Since I never returned to live in Connecticut, talking with my mother from afar became a time-worn tradition. Most phone conversations ended up being the same:

"Hi, Mom. It's Ralph."

This simple salutation would trigger her pent-up storehouse of information, updates, and opinions. She was like a volcano spewing lava in all directions. The amazing thing was how she could flow from one subject to the next—a completely different topic, without a pause or a breath.

"Uh huh." I usually volunteered this unsolicited response, so she would feel at home, like it was with my dad. Believing she had cinched my interest, this only launched her into another flurry of hot-winded anecdotes.

Sometimes I asked a brief question or provided something rhetorical: "Is that a fact?" But honestly, saying anything else never really seemed necessary.

In my thirties and beyond, when family and job duties were particularly pressing, I would approach our conversations with this same pattern. Then I literally would put the phone down for five or ten minutes and do chores—take out the dog, go to the bathroom, finish balancing my checkbook. When I returned, I'd hear my dear sweet mother still cranking along.

"Well, Mom. It's been nice talking with you."

"And as I told your father—"

"Great, Mom. Okay." I would try to wrap up the call, but her words were endless. "Bye, now. Call you soon." Inevitably, I would hang up with a sigh. I'm not proud of these moments, but I did it to survive.

My mother can suck the life out of a room, and at the time I wasn't entirely sure of her power through a phone line.

When I moved my parents close to me, I still called, but now many of our conversations occurred while driving to the store or in person over a meal. At forty-five miles per hour or before the dinner check arrives, there really is no escape.

On one such evening, I took her to buy groceries. During the trip home, she talked, as usual, about an incident that happened about a hundred years ago—okay, about sixty years—the eventful yet disappointing visit with Aunt Edna in 1955. It is one of those topics, unforgettable and unforgivable, that always provoked some type of singularly passionate eruption in my mother.

After we dropped off the groceries, I suggested we go for a bite to eat. As we drove to one of the few restaurants that didn't spur a complaint or criticism from my mother, I swallowed wrong somehow. I was not popping an antacid. I was not chewing gum or slurping soda.

I just breathed, then swallowed, and suddenly was choking. My chest rumbled. Tears streamed down my face. I coughed and wheezed and tried to catch my breath.

During my red-faced stupor, we could have crashed. I could have suffocated and died. Yet my mother remained oblivious. I wiped the sweat from my forehead and hacked up phlegm, trying to see beyond my steamed-up glasses. I finally slowed the car and rolled to a dead stop in the middle of an empty street. And my mother still prattled on ...

I leaned past her and popped the glove compartment to

grab another napkin to help contain my coughing throat and spitting.

Suddenly, my mother paused and looked straight at me. "Can you believe it? After all these years, that's what she said to me. Well, I can tell you, that was the last time ..."

I returned her gaze, stunned. There were just no words.

So why did my mother never acknowledge or even notice I was asphyxiating? I don't know. Why do the good die young? Why is there so much suffering in the world? Why? is a question she doesn't like to answer.

Despite my mother's prolific use of words for ... well, everything ... one question she refuses to answer is, "Who is my biological father?" She refuses to tell me his name, how she met him, or any detail large or small about the man.

It was not until fifty years later, as I proceeded with plans to move her to California and was tossing old newspapers and rummaging through old documents that I discovered a possible clue: "Edward Matin, Army Corps of Engineers." I know my mother served in the Army Corps of Engineers when she was young. *Maybe this Edward is my father?* My heart thumped. *Maybe she met him there?*

I dug deeper into this box and many others, primed to find something, anything else. Then I uncovered divorce papers between Edward Matin and Louise Matin. *My mother was married? My mother was married, possibly to my biological father!* She'd had this whole other life about which I know nothing. It was impossible to fathom. And she repeatedly refused to corroborate anything.

No matter how much I begged, pleaded, or shouted, my mother deflected, diverged, and simply clammed up. I sank into a chair. How it is possible to always talk and never say anything?

I snapped from my memory when we finally arrived at the restaurant. During dinner, my mother griped about the peas and how "nothing is done right anymore."

"Uh huh." As my throat felt soothed by warm, buttery mashed potatoes, my mind drifted. This time it was to my dad. He was gone but still here. Alive in my head.

We were in my childhood home. It was summer during one of my quick fly-by visits. I squeezed in a really big project during the few days I was in town. I have no siblings, and this time I felt it deeply because I needed help.

I rented a chainsaw, pulled out both large and small clippers, and tackled the three hundred feet of trees and thick bushes that line my parents' driveway and the entire east edge of the property. Years ago, my dad planted this irregular row of saplings. Now it's a jungle that rivals Amazonia. I can say this without exaggerating because I've trekked through Amazonia. My dad sought to provide a privacy buffer to the neighbor's adjacent house.

I labored and dripped sweat for two days. My arms and fingers grew numb, rife with cuts and bruises from dragging sections of knotted foliage to a massive compost pile in the farthest corner of the property. By the end, the pile was twice my height.

Afterward, though dead tired, I showered and dressed

and packed my parents into the car to treat them to their favorite Italian dinner. I drove, and my dad rode shotgun, staring ahead without a word. My mother sat in back, her mouth cruising faster than the capable speed of the car. As we drifted slowly down their driveway, I couldn't help myself. I admired my handiwork through the side window. What used to be an unending mass of wild limbs with mangled leaves and mottled branches was now a straight edge of green, trim and even.

Wow, that really came out nice. I smiled to myself. Seeing this transformation made me happy to have squeezed in this mammoth task in such a short, busy visit. However, neither my mom nor dad turned their head or even appeared to notice the new landscape, let alone say anything. No nod, no grin. No lifted eyebrow of thanks for spending two full days trying to make their yard more presentable. I glanced at my mother in the rearview mirror, prattling.

"Can you believe it?" she said. "After all these years, that's what she said to me. Well, I can tell you, that was the last time—"

I looked at my dad—his eyes straight ahead, blissfully hard of hearing. That day they said so much to me, without a single word.

I don't know what it's like to face caring for elderly parents with brothers or sisters in the mix, but I have friends who vouch it can be as challenging as my own situation—just in different ways. Sometimes everyone in the family is talking at once, and siblings disagree—ferociously.

One of my friends was willing to share her story. She is a registered nurse and came from a family with eight children. Her mother was suffering from late-stage polycythemia vera (cancer in the bone marrow). When it came time for her mom to enter hospice, it was generally agreed among the siblings that my friend was the most logical choice to provide in-home care. Together with her husband and teenage son, she established an open-door policy so the rest of the family could visit all through the day and evening. They even set up an extra single bed for whoever was with their mom during the night shift.

Since I have no brothers or sisters, this arrangement sounded heavenly to me. Lots of people to do everything. Lots of help to provide 24/7 emotional support. But just because everyone in her family was willing to help didn't keep old patterns of conflict from bubbling up to cause problems.

My friend explained that appropriate conversations did take place in advance about her mom's care. Her four brothers were content to let most of the decision-making come from the four sisters, which was a blessing. The problem was the four sisters couldn't agree on much! In reality, it was more like three against one. One sister was always fighting against the majority. Of course she wanted to see her mom get well. So she would bring over unusual drinks, iron-rich foods, and other alternative medicines for her mom to try. This food was hard for her mom to eat and drink, yet her sister would insist her mom consume it. The mom, not wanting to offend her daughter, asked my friend to talk with her sister. She didn't know how to say no to her daughter. My friend would usually get her other two sisters involved, and it would soon turn into an argument. The one sister then would accuse the other three of not loving their mother.

As the weeks and months of hospice turned into a year, my friend turned into a 24/7 supervising caregiver and struggled to balance the care for her own family. As the stress amplified, so did her mother's will to live. One day her mom decided she didn't like her hair and wanted a permanent. My friend expressed her desperate thought: "Really? I thought she was in the process of dying. How long is this going to take?"

Since her sister-in-law was a hairdresser, one afternoon they gave their mom a permanent in the kitchen, which in and of itself is a simple process. But because of the sibling tension it turned into a huge and complicated undertaking. It was the spark that caused the explosion.

My friend told me they have anger management issues in her family. A single sentence can turn into a full-scale war in less than a minute. It seemed there were no healthy discussions in her family, only forceful statements of fact or opinion. Words were misinterpreted, feelings were hurt, grudges were held, and apologies were never given or accepted.

When my friend's one sister took the first step to tell their dying mother something all the siblings had decided but had not yet mentioned, another sister intervened. She told her to stop and put a hand on her sister's shoulder. Since that sister was never one to be physically restrained, she pushed back.

Muscles tensed, a little more force was used, and one sister's hands ended up around the other's neck, choking her.

My friend and her fourth sister were there in an instant. Words flew. "Stop pushing." "Move out of the way." "Get your hands off me." "Leave her alone." One sister got down on her knees, hands folded, pleading for them to stop fighting. Begging them to stop. By now my friend had her hands around her initiating sister's neck, demanding that she let go of sister number three.

My friend described the ugly look on her face but also the knowledge that while her hands were loose around her sister's neck, she knew they wouldn't get any tighter. As the tension eventually subsided, each set of fighting sisters released the other. Fight over.

But the one sister never forgot. She would always remember my friend's hands around her neck, even though my friend asked her forgiveness. "It will be a long time, if ever, that she will forgive me for all these hurtful things," my friend lamented. "We used to be quite close, used to run, work out, and train for triathlons together." She concluded, "I've always known that my sister was difficult to live with, and she would probably say the same about me, but I still miss her nearly every day."

The stress of caring for an elderly parent can push us to do things we never thought ourselves capable of doing. If you were to meet my friend, you would find her caring, nurturing, and professional. Her mom raised her children to be independent and intelligent, with strong wills to forge ahead in an often challenging and difficult world. I know because I recognize these same traits in me—and in my mother.

My mother often makes forceful statements. She was independent, smart, strong-willed, even daring for a woman of her age and generation. Of her own initiative and funding she attended "radio" school in Chicago and the University of Laval in Montreal. Can you imagine my mother as a deejay? With her mouth, I believe she could have done it. She traveled to Bermuda as part of a bucket list and had many other goals, but there were few professional opportunities for women in that era.

For my mother, words became one of her few outlets for wielding power. They were her sword for surviving physical abuse from her father, for tending to tremendous emotional scars to try not to feel a victim to those around her or to anyone ever again. The Bible often talks about how the mouth is a two-edged sword with the power to bless or curse, to edify or destroy. I think my mother sees it as "destroy" or "be destroyed."

It is likely that I got my thirst for travel and drive to accomplish goals from my mother. I am fascinated by communication—how and why people of distinct cultures talk and where their deep conversations take place. I admit, I contribute my fair share of words to the world each day. I am acutely aware that we are all creatures subject to heredity and shaped by our environment. This is a big reason why I notice how my mother is always talking. I do not want to end up like her.

Interspersed amidst all her complaints, I try to remember the sage and encouraging things she has said to me, the special words that kept me going in moments of uncertainty and confusion. When the road ahead seemed especially challenging , she would say, "Ralph, you can do anything you put your mind to!" or "Believe in yourself and never give up!" and "God said, 'I know what's up ahead better than you. So trust me.'"

Someday my mother will stop talking. When I think about it, the sound of silence will be deafening.

Chapter 6

Mama, Please Don't Say That Again

I would often wonder why Mama always got her way when we were kids. Even if we ignored her, somehow whatever she wanted was how life turned out. It seemed like some mysterious magic, a golden gift from God. Now that I'm older, I realize there's nothing supernatural about Mama's ability. I know it's just that there really is something to the old adage, "The squeaky wheel gets the grease." In Mama's case, the one who says the same thing one hundred times gets the job done quickly.

Mama is a true pro. She'll call your name, calmly yet without stopping, until you answer. Sometimes you just don't hear her, and if it that's the case she'll go from a very low octave to a high screeching voice that feels like a teacher's nails scraping the blackboard for students' attention. It doesn't matter if you're in the bathroom—busy, if you know what I mean—or in the middle of a timely work requirement. Mama will relentlessly repeat your name until you not only answer but appear before her in person, if you happen to be over for a visit.

Then she'll say in a very sweet voice that no one can refuse, "Could you please get me some water?" or "Can I have the telephone, dear? I'd like you to order something from the catalog," or some other question that probably could've waited and didn't merit the never-ending twang of your name through the halls of the house.

Since Mama isn't super mobile, she doesn't go shopping in the store anymore. She has become a catalog queen. When she feels she needs something, she'll sift through the pages, fold the corner of the sheet that has what she prizes, and then call you "to do some ordering." Although I don't mind being her home-shopping assistant, sometimes I feel a little wary when I call Mama and hear the request.

"Hi, Mama. How are you?"

"Fine, baby. I got some ordering for you to do."

"Sure," I say. "I'm a little busy right now, but I'll do it when I can."

"Good, baby. Thank you. Because I really need some things I found in the catalog."

"So how are you feeling today?"

"Okay." She says it, but I'm not quite sure she means it.

"I'm coming for dinner."

"That's nice." Then there's the pause.

"What would you like to eat? Are you starting to get hungry?"

"You know what I'm hungry for? To get this ordering done."

At some point in every conversation from the time she makes her request and the moment the ordering gets done, she'll mention it I don't know how many times, just intermittently, during the same chat. It doesn't matter the topic. She does this not just with me but with my sisters, until one of us arrives to the house and places the order.

It's the same way with food. Mama doesn't cook anymore, so my sisters and I take turns bringing her food. I usually tend to do the cooking and put meals in containers to be eaten during the week. My oldest sister brings her something to eat from her favorite food spots. Sometimes it's steak. Sometimes it's shrimp. Sometimes steak and shrimp. Once you bring food from a place she really enjoys, it doesn't matter what's in the house. Mama is going to ask for that food. It's just like the ordering. She'll ask and ask and keep asking until you bring her that food.

Sometimes I'm tempted not to bring her what she's calling for just to see how many times she'll call my name.

"Feebee."

"One ..."

"Feebee."

"Two ..."

"Feebee?"

"Three ..."

"Feebee. Feebee. Feebee ..."

But I don't. She'd probably just wear me out anyway. If

Mama needs someone to file papers or hang clothes or a gardener to hack weeds, trim a tree, pick fruit, she flips into request mode until the task gets done—and done to her liking.

Mama is slick without even knowing it. Sometimes she'll present her request seemingly on the sly. She isn't dishonest. The woman is just a natural expert at reading situations. Usually, it goes something like this:

"I sure wish I had some vanilla ice cream or ginger snap cookies."

"Mama, do you want me to get some for you?"

"Oh no, baby. Don't bother."

Her smile twinkles. Her eyes crinkle with gratitude that you heard her the first time. She says no. She says not to bother. But I find my legs carrying me into the kitchen. My hands scoop vanilla ice cream and ginger snaps into a bowl, and I bring it to her. And here's the irony: she is never surprised when I return with whatever she wants.

I don't deal with most people this way. I'm more direct. So these situations can really get on my nerves, if I let them. I'm not only direct, but I prefer to get things done fast. This is why it's easy to remember how difficult it can be for such a speedy woman to be slowed down by age. When my back aches, I sympathize for how hard it must be for an active little bee like Mama, who is used to helping others, now to wait for others to help her. I see how rising from a chair, strolling to the kitchen, and walking back carefully with a full cup of coffee can be such a challenge.

Getting things done fast isn't the one thing Mama and

I have in common. We're both the youngest of our siblings and, I'm not too proud to admit, a little spoiled. Like Mama, if I want something, I want it *right now*. We also both have large, capable hands and big feet. A deep love for children and family is the center of our lives.

To tell the truth, I've been known to repeat myself multiple times to gain the quick attention of unruly kids. It might seem like a hundred times to them too. So now that I'm older and able to see how much I'm like Mama, I realize we both have needs and do the best we can to meet them.

I even understand how all those years ago Mama always seemed to get her way with my dad. After fifty-four years of marriage, it was just easier to honor her request, whatever it was, the first time, just so Mama wouldn't say it again. At least this is the way it seemed until my sisters and I started caring full time for Mama.

Simply by living as long as she has, Mama is teaching me how life is a marathon and not a sprint. It's important to enjoy and appreciate it as much as we can, because we're in it for the long haul. Mama's ability to ask for what she needs over and over again is simply a sign of life. She is alive, and even amid moments that drive me crazy, I'm glad she is.

Maybe, just maybe, my dad swooped in to help her so quickly because he loved her so much and wanted her to be happy. I say this because, today, I see my sisters and me doing the same.

Chapter 7

When Parent Becomes Child

"They're too stupid to know they're stupid." This is what my mother says to me about her fellow guests in the lockdown unit of the Alzheimer's and dementia side of her retirement facility.

I break out laughing until my eyes are tearing. "Mom, that's one of the funniest things I have ever heard!" She grins with a simultaneously devious and empty expression. She knows she has scored big with this one.

When I moved my mother from Connecticut, I never expected to be here with her. *In this place.* Now when I look back at all her craziness, I can see how we were headed here the whole time.

In the background are many noises. One lady constantly repeats, "Safe and sound. Tut, tut, tut. I'm safe and sound." There is always a musical track from an old movie playing, too loudly. An audio pacifier. And when someone punches in the code to come into the complex but doesn't close the gate fast enough, there is an abrupt alarm that blazes through our ears.

"This place is crazy," my mother reminds me again.

"Well, you look pretty good. How is it going?" I try to sound cheerful.

"I dunno."

Once each weekend, I visit my mother during her breakfast period. During these times I have come to know the people around her. Lillian is at the table with her eyes closed, mumbling numbers or repeating, "Sit quietly and wait for breakfast." Freeda, always smiling benignly, sports her French beret. There is Violet, constantly giggling at nothing and talking gibberish. Isabel hovers near the coded entry gate trying to get out. Rosario, with a disgusted harrumph on her face, rips her napkin into multiple squares and arranges them into some pattern that obviously means something to her.

Then there are the ones who were professionals in life. Gene talks boisterously and always asks, "*Where* is my coffee?" Juliette perpetually pulls her wheelchair around by her heels, always going nowhere in a hurry. John walks around cursing and grunting, and Agnes meanders silently. I recently met Sandra, who told me she used to be a sheriff. She constantly repeats, "It's forty below zero in here!" and is a quick draw to cuff the hand of any care worker who tries to move her walker. Then there is Martha, a former ballroom dance competitor. She is motionless at the moment but can hold her head up high and still move with grace.

It is in the commonality of their circumstances, knowing

that each one of them was a totally vibrant person—an active parent, a successful businessperson, a creative engineer—that I see my mother in a different light. The dwindling light of who these people are illuminates my understanding of her.

As we sit with occasional conversation, I think about the past. Our past. I try to remember what was important to me when I was eighteen. When I was fifty. What was so important last month? A job? Promotion? Someone who offended me? Politics? Who won the World Series? Sitting here I realize how I respond to life too intensely and with a serious nature. Sometimes we just have to laugh or crumble into a thousand pieces from grief.

I typically visit my mother on Saturdays. Most of the time, like today, it is for a ninety-minute block centered around breakfast. I usually arrive near 7:00 a.m. when the night shift is leaving and the day crew is just getting started. Both are sleepy, for different reasons. When I enter the complex, most of the residents, except those prone to wander, are sitting in the common area, either in seats or their wheelchairs. Today's distraction is a western movie. It is nearly summer and everyone has been dressed in anticipation of a warm day, but most of the clients, including my mother, are cold. The air conditioning and ceiling fans make it feel like another season entirely.

With a quiet sweeping gesture, I customarily bend my knee in front of her. It is the only way I can make eye contact, since she is hunched over in her wheelchair, staring at nothing really but appearing to scrutinize the floor. Her back straightens, shoulders stretch to full width, and a seldom-seen smile lights up her face.

"Hi, Mom," I say. "It looks like you're still kicking."

"Yep, I guess I am still kicking."

I marvel at how everything has changed in just one year. It seems like yesterday my mother was making her special pot roast, lasagna, summer squash, and berry pies. Even though it had been at least ten years since my mother cooked me a meal—and believe me, I miss it—at least she was still ambulatory, fully functional in her weird way, and preparing her own food on a daily basis. But her food choices had devolved into a very peculiar selection—and it had to be specific items.

Every week we would buy the same three or four varieties of a particular brand of frozen meal, fruit cup, Hawaiian sweet rolls, coffee, breakfast loaf cakes, and Entenmann's chocolate-covered donuts. I literally have driven to five different grocery stores in a single day to find those donuts.

"Oh, I don't want to put you out of your way, son," my mother would say with a sigh. "But they are so delicious. I only have one left. If I cut it in half, it will last me until Monday."

"Don't worry, Mom. I'll take care of it." *What else could I say?* I like to travel, but this isn't what I had in mind. I guess when you start pushing ninety, it's easy to fixate on the favorites. Life is short.

So I started spending more time in the grocery store. It seems that as she aged, I would find my mother cutting everything into pieces. If we bought a pre-made turkey sandwich, she would cut it into four mini-sandwiches and eat one every day. If we bought a chocolate bar, it had to be the bite-size ones or else she'd nibble one square at a time. She would get full on one-third of a frozen dinner. I was amazed. I could down three of those things and still be hungry.

Although it happened over time, it's easy to see how my mother could dwindle to the ninety pounds that now sit in her wheelchair. Bringing my mother to this place was a gradual realization that turned into a fast decision. I would be asleep and suddenly awake to my mother shouting, "Who's watching me in the bathroom?" or "I hear someone cursing in French!"

Except this time it was getting serious. It was no longer just an inconvenience or an irritation. This new challenge had reached the same level of intensity as losing my spouse to divorce and watching our firstborn daughter die at ten years old from a degenerative neurological disease. My mother's behavior was bizarre, and something had to be done.

My mother had always been a bit strange, so at first it was hard to tell the "new weird" from the "normal weird." She had sensitive ears, but now she obsessed over simple noises, like someone slamming a cupboard. She started hearing and seeing things, like the day she told me, "The floor opened up."

I couldn't live with it anymore, so I moved my mother into assisted living. Within days, the doctors had diagnosed her with dementia.

Caring for my mother at home helped me appreciate

the senior care workers at her facility. Most earn close to minimum wage. They feed and clothe my mother, change her diapers, brush her hair. I think of tipping them, because I'm so grateful for the hard work they do. The need for elderly care providers is increasing massively, perhaps by more than 50 percent in the next decade according to projections by the Bureau of Labor Statistics.

Journeying with my mother, I've had the opportunity to enter into a new world. I am now part of an invisible culture—the culture of the aging. It is one of those things that we can't know what it's like until we're there. It reminds me of the journey I traveled with my firstborn daughter, when I discovered a world of parents coping with terminally ill children. There are needles and surgeries and unavoidable sadness.

You might think this experience with my daughter would have prepared me for the journey with my mother. But it didn't. When we are parents, our children remain our children—no matter how old they are. The second they are born, we suddenly are ready to sacrifice our lives for them. When a parent becomes a child, how are we supposed to feel? How do we cope?

We stay balanced emotionally, physically, and relationally—or at least we try. I am not like Feager, who is great at self-care. She goes to movies, attends concerts, and makes time for parties and extended family gatherings. Sometimes she recharges her batteries by just relaxing with veggies and watching reality TV. When Feager shared this with me, I shook my head and laughed.

"Being with my mother is too much of a dose of reality for me," I told her. "She is like a TV show I can't turn off. I wish I could just point the remote at her and click mute."

This was during the height of my frustration, when being with my mother meant 24/7 care and always being available as her emotional and physical anchor to a healthy reality. However, even then I managed to snag an hour to read a book or magazine to know what was going on in the world. Sometimes I would escape to a nearby beach. For a few precious moments, I would recline in my folding chair and watch the waves, relaxing with a seven-inch cigar to clear my mind.

Today at my mother's facility there is a celebration outside in the courtyard. It is decorated with balloons and streamers. There is even a live singer in a barber shop vest and striped hat, playing an electric piano and singing popular tunes from the 1930s and '40s.

This weekend about twenty residents with family and friends gather to honor all birthdays older than ninety, as well as Mother's Day. The staff hand the high-achievers a rose, commemoration certificate, strawberries, and a cupcake—starting with the youngest, and culminating with Millie, who is 105.

My other two daughters, now adults, are in attendance. My mother grins, and her eyes sparkle at all the fuss everyone makes over her. Afterward, we sit and chat, like a family. The girls visit with Grandma and I soak it in, glad to see three important women in my life all smiling at the same time.

Then one of my daughters ventures to ask the question. *That question.* "So, Grandma. Tell us. Who is Dad's biological father?" They ask, trying one last time.

I can feel my heart start pumping hard. Hoping.

My mother inhales. She looks each one of us in the face. My eyes grow wide. My gaze meets hers. She is lucid. She opens her lips to speak. But only an unintentionally feeble response flows out to us.

My face begins to burn. Her refusal, or maybe now her inability to answer still riles me.

Why won't she just tell me?

Sometimes I wonder if she decided not to tell me because of the way we met my adopted dad. We were at the park, and he was sitting on a bench. I sat down right next to him and then snuggled up. He smiled at me as if we belonged together. Essentially, I played matchmaker for my parents at five years old.

My daughters stand and lean over to give my mother their good-byes with kisses and hugs. I end this visit with my mother in the way that has become our new tradition. I wheel her chair outside to listen to the birds and the water fountain. Then I take both hands to pull her up to stretch her bones and muscles a bit, because I know she has been sitting for too long. My mother clings to me, with her head against my chest.

"I love you, son," she whispers.

Then suddenly it makes sense. Not all of it. Just enough to help me move on from today.

Chapter 8

What's Wrong with Mom?

Mama has always been here. She's the one constant in my life. Someone I can depend on, someone who cares about every inch of me. She's like peace and comfort after a hard day.

I remember when I still lived at home. Mama would keep the house warm in winter and cool in summer. Sweet aromas welcomed me whenever I walked through the door. To this day I still keep candles and aromatic plug-ins throughout the house. They're a simple thing, but this small act lifts me even after a grueling day and grinding commute through LA traffic.

Mama always prepared a warm meal for me and my sisters. There was even a hot breakfast every morning, so we'd be alert throughout the day. When I think of our takeout culture in a world of fast food, I am amazed at how hard Mama worked to do this for us. She was never too weary to pepper the meal with funny faces when sharing with us some goofy story that happened to her during the day.

No matter how hard she worked, Mama kept her sense of humor. Laughter often rang throughout the house. King Solomon says that laughter is like medicine. Funny, we seldom needed to go to the doctor.

Mama never left dishes in the sink at night. "Never know when someone may stop by," she'd say. From early morning to late evening, Mama was always ready for visitors.

She insisted we eat dinner together as a family. Communicating was always open. It was over fried chicken, collard greens, and peach cobbler that my sisters and I learned to talk with one another—and this, probably more anything, has helped us stay tight as a family today. All of our giggles at that dinner table paved the way, and there was always an extra chair for whomever dropped by and wanted to join in.

Getting together and laughing is something our entire family does. We're all so close. I love all my cousins, their spouses, and little ones as if they were my own. All of us are grown and have jobs and ministries. We're busy folk, but we manage to get together for barbecues and special events. Four generations huddled together—talking and catching up, eating and laughing too much at a cousin's joke or a child's smile. Mama shakes her head at our disorganized chatting, tries to protect us from ourselves, but we all know she relishes these moments. She can't hide her grins. Someone notices, makes her laugh. Then her love spills out.

None of us would ever dream of putting our seniors into

a convalescent facility, though I understand why people do. But for us, it's not who we are and not the way we were taught. From the time we were young, we watched our parents caring for their parents in our home right up until the end, no matter how bad it got. And now, we do the same.

My cousin is a medical doctor. You'd think having a doctor plus five siblings in the family might help when it comes to caring for my aging auntie. Not in my cousin's case.

My uncle died very tragically in a hit and run while crossing the street one night, when my cousin was just a teenager. Her mother was faced with raising six children by herself. She was strong and courageous. The woman was a rock. She worked hard, with a mind set tougher than bricks. She managed to put all six children through college and trade schools. And she did all this while living in the South in the 1960s. Some of the kids, like my cousin, received scholarships. But for the most part, my aunt hammered self-sufficiency into them and made sure they could take good care of themselves.

Tragedy after tragedy struck my cousin's family. But my aunt hunkered down, stayed straight as a nail, and weathered it all. How did she do it? She clung to God. She hugged Him hard when faced with the death of her own mother, who had helped her when my uncle died. She held on tighter after discovering her oldest son had multiple sclerosis and even when she had to bury one of her daughters after losing the battle against cancer.

After so much loss, my cousin says her mom began to lose that spark. "Her eyes no longer had a glow. They became very hollow. My mother got very hard, even harder than she normally was." My cousin watched as the woman she'd loved since birth became distant, less talkative, forgetful, and even accusatory.

One day my cousin told me her mother took a drive and some stranger had to call them, because my aunt didn't know where she was. Another day, my cousin said her mom was accusing her kids of rearranging her belongings behind her back, breaking into her safe deposit box, and stealing money. "Just wild insane things, which we would never do!" my cousin insisted.

By now my cousin and her siblings are caring for my aunt full time while trying to take care of the daily needs of their own families. They do it because this is the woman who gave them life so they could have the blessed benefits they now enjoy.

Then one day, my cousin sends me an e-mail. I could just tell you what she said, but there's no way for me to capture her desperate words. There's no way for me to communicate how my heart reached out to my cousin's heart when I read them. Here's a little of what she wrote:

> She called the police on my sister, who is the medical doctor. My sister called and said ... "Mom has called the police on me" ... I said ... "Do you want me to come over?" ... She says ... "Mom has called the police on me!"

When I got to the house, my sister was distraught and crying because our mother, who she cared for, built a house for, gave money to, and did everything for called the police on her for stealing! And there was the police, my sister, my mother and a lot of grief and sadness. WHAT IS WRONG WITH MOTHER?

For my cousin, the D word wasn't death. It was dementia. There was nothing "wrong" with my aunt, but in these moments, my aunt is gone. The woman who was isn't there anymore. My cousin has to face that her mom has drifted away, like her grandmother so many years ago. My cousin says the emptiness in her mother's eyes becomes more prevalent. It seems little by little the disappointments, disasters, and tragedies kept carving out a piece of her until nothing was left. Her body is present, but inside there is just confusion and emptiness. The family she spent a lifetime cherishing are now strangers.

When something like this happens, it's hard—the hardest part of someone's aging process. You might think it's hardest on the elderly person who suffers the confusion of chaos and life shifting so suddenly. However, sometimes I wonder if the pain is greater for those left behind, like being chained to a smelly couch and forced to watch an awful never-ending reality TV show.

For my cousins, it was just too much. The one who wrote

me the e-mail died from a heart attack earlier this year, and my other cousin, the doctor, just collapsed from a massive heart trauma last week. Meanwhile, my aunt lives on, with more grief to add to her book of misery and even greater reason to fade from this realm we're living in. True to our family nature, the other cousins have shifted to pick up the caretaking slack and are trying not to overtax one another.

I think about this as I light a relaxing candle and settle into an overstuffed easy chair across from Mama. Thank God that for some, mind-altering diseases never come. These seniors are like my mama, still feisty and giving orders about how and when and where they want their lives to happen.

But there are certain moments when I see Mama sad or unusually quiet or barely touching her food. I worry. I take her in my arms, hug her tight, and whisper, "Live, please!" My sisters do the same. Mama sparkles and smiles. She kisses our cheek, rubs our back like when were small girls, because she knows how much we still need her. She knows we never want to let her go.

My sisters and I were given all we needed and most of what we wanted. We were shown love throughout our lifetime. This is why my oldest sister keeps the house warm in winter and cool in summer and smelling with sweet aromas. It's why my other sister does Mama's washing and cleaning and gets her to church on time. It's why I work with doctors to tend to her medicine and keep track of appointments, talk to her by phone three times a day, and bring her whatever warm meal she wants.

It's also why we never leave dishes in the sink at night. Because even today, you never quite know who will drop by to visit Mama. It may be someone hungry for her smile or needing a comforting hand after a hard day. I look at Zenobia, the one who lives with Mama 24/7.

"Go take a bubble bath, Little Mama."

My sister shoots me a weird look. She doesn't like people giving her orders—none of us do.

"Do something nice for yourself," I tell her.

She hears the insistence in my voice and wrinkles her nose at me. I scrunch my face and stick out my tongue at her. She laughs and strolls toward the tub to run her bathwater. I sigh, so glad to see that she does.

Chapter 9

Mama's Ten Commandments

When my sisters and I were children, Mama had what seemed a never-ending list of advice. They were more tidbits than full-blown lectures—although I got plenty of those too. One thing that has stuck in my mind over the years is when she would say, "Feebee, always make sure you have on clean panties without holes."

Sometimes Dianne, Zenobia, and I would roll our eyes, depending on how old we were at the time, but in the end we always giggled about it. Now Mama is much too dignified, gracious, and kind to say something like this in public. She would never embarrass us and openly declare her clean panties rule in public. But underneath all that grace hides a bundle of fun that we like to pull out of Mama whenever we can.

I think about all of this today as Dianne, Zenobia, and I visit with cousins. Mama sits primly, nodding and dispensing her tidbits of knowledge. Like she usually does. At this gathering it's just us women. We're family. We're close. We love one another. And we appreciate good humor.

So I share Mama's panty commandment and grin at all the happy laughter it brings. But Mama, clever as she is, just smiles and smoothes her blouse with a dainty hand. I see the expression on her face.

"You sayin' I have dirty drawers?"

I lift an eyebrow at her. "Who has dirty drawers?"

My cousins join in the fun. They erupt into another round of giggles and wink at me and Mama.

"Look here, I'm still the Mama and—"

"Oh, Eloise!" My oldest sister grins and hugs her.

Mama hates it when we call her Eloise. But gazing at all the joyful faces, even she can't stifle her own laughter. "Like I said. I'm the *Mama*!"

I give her "the look," but it only fuels her.

"Ever been in an accident on your way anywhere?" she asks with a straight face.

I have. But this is not the reason why I'm wearing clean underwear. I don't live in fear. I'm not afraid of crashing my car and paramedics seeing faded, dreary drawers. It's because this woman in her own strange and loving way makes a good point. I've come to discover that Mama is an unexpected sage.

Still, there are so many things she has done over the years that are just … well, weird. When I was younger I used to ask myself, "Why does Mama *say that*?" Now that I'm an auntie and great-auntie to so many cousins and children, I understand. I find myself leaning over to my goddaughter and saying, "Don't drink milk and laugh. It might come out your nose."

When I got older, I noticed Mama used a shaver. "Always shave your pubic hair," she'd say.

What on earth for? I thought. Now I know ... to make those gray hairs disappear.

Every night she'd slather lotion on her body and cream on her face before going to bed. Now at ninety-three, she has the smoothest skin, hasn't got a wrinkle, and always looks refreshed.

"Eat your vegetables."

"Drink your water."

"Ride your bike."

"Walk around the block."

"Balance your checkbook to the penny."

"Never leave dishes in the sink at night. Never know who might stop by."

Good habits produce a good life. Mama's mantras march through my mind every day. Without thinking, I reach for the carrots instead of potato chips. I monitor my finances like a hawk and never spend beyond my means. I try to carry a water bottle everywhere. And right beside that in my purse is a small, portable fan so I can stay fresh and cool (you'd have one too, to survive summers in Los Angeles).

Today I look at my clean kitchen sink and then at Mama, knowing she's the reason for it all. Right now, it's after dinner and everyone is full. Mama sits in the living room in a large chair holding court. Women of all ages gather around. Surprise visitors arrive, hoping to hear her speak.

Self-care is still important to Mama. Not just the outside, but the inside. She glances at her listeners. A little sigh escapes her lips. She grins and gears up. "Don't follow the crowd. Let the crowd follow you. No one in this entire world is better than you!"

Mama's words have bounced around my head my whole life. This is probably why I'm not easily intimidated by anyone and have always gotten the job or promotion. I've learned to say what I mean and mean what I say. But my words sometimes get me into trouble.

Not Mama. We never saw her do too much arguing. "Sometimes it's better to keep quiet for peace sake." When we clashed, I would often wonder, *Whose peace? Certainly not mine.* This wisdom is probably how my parents managed to stay happily married for fifty-four years. There is a great balance between speaking, listening, and just being plain quiet.

So when Mama educates me about clean panties—even though I've had my own AARP card for more than a decade—I don't argue. I just shrug, or maybe I smile. I try to appreciate that she's still here to teach according to the Book of Eloise.

"Be nice to your sisters" was always at the top of her list. Part of working together to take care of Mama means not ratting on one another and causing an elderly woman to worry. My sisters and I try to resolve disagreements while they're still minor frustrations, instead of letting them build into monstrous walls of no communication. You know with siblings you're going to have conflict, so it's no use in being surprised when such things happen.

You might think that making sure Mama gets her meds or goes to the doctor is the most important care we can offer her. But this isn't the case. For Mama, peace among her children is what feeds her soul and her happiness. So my sisters and I try to give her that first. In the process, we have discovered that everything else falls into place more easily when we focus on compassion, grace, and speaking calmly and openly with one another.

I admit, this isn't always easy for any of us. But I do it because I want to enjoy every moment with my mom.

You see, I'm the youngest and haven't had as much time with Mama as my sisters. I try not to think of her leaving this earth, although I know it's coming. I know it will happen.

I've already lived through the sudden death of my father. I've counseled and prayed with parishioners through their loss of loved ones. But Mama has always been here with me. Even though I know she's going to heaven, and I'll see her there someday, nothing can replace a mom's love.

I can't bear to think of when she won't be here anymore.

She's healthy.

She's far from "that."

At least for now.

Chapter 10

The D Word

Moms are a force of nature. They birth us, sustain us with their own bodies for the first years of life, and seem to control our worlds for the next twenty years. We never escape the wind of their words, the sparkle of their smiles, or their tears of disappointment. They feed us, dress us, worry over us, and send us into our futures with both relief and sorrow.

Who our mothers are and what they do, no matter how crazy, just seems normal.

This is why it's so difficult for me when my mother scooches close and whispers, "Someone tried to kill me last night."

"Oh really, how?" I lean back and cross my legs.

"They shot me."

"Where did they shoot you?"

"Right here." She points to the middle of her chest.

When I ask her where the bullets are, she looks at me as if I'm stupid.

"They went right through."

Of course, because everything always goes right through—especially when you live 24/7 in a dementia unit.

My mother's words always went "right through," sniping my heart in a clean shot. So I know how much it can hurt when you're killed. Although my mother's words come from a confused brain, I understand her. I even sympathize. Facing death can be unsettling, especially while you're still alive. Nobody likes to talk about the D word.

I grab a chair and sit next to her. I pat her cheek. My arms scoop her frail body into a bear hug. I rub that spot on the back of her neck that relaxes her and try to ease the stress of having been shot. Her translucent skin is cold. In forty-five minutes breakfast will be served. Unlocking the two safety bars on her wheelchair, I move my mother into the dining area. I lean down within earshot.

"Would you like me to get your sweater?" I ask, already knowing the response.

"Oh yes, I would like that very much. Thank you." Then she adds something extra, which surprises me. "You are the best son!"

I secure the key to her room from an attendant and return with her favorite blue sweater. After helping her into it, I fasten each button and pat her cheek again. I remember how she used to do this to me when I was a young boy. I give her a little finger massage on her neck and upper back. Her smile turns into a sunrise.

"Oh, that feels so good," she coos.

We exchange the usual banter. I make a remark about preparing for her one hundredth birthday party, although today it does not seem to me that this century benchmark will arrive. Mom looks worn this morning. Her eyes are red and rheumy. A few more whiskers seem to have grown on her chin. I decide to slip a note and $10 into the mailbox of the manicurist just so she can clean her fingers and paint her nails to make them more presentable. I take my mother's frail hands in mine and examine them. They are bent with age and arthritis.

While carrying on the conversation with my mother, I laugh often and try to keep her as animated as possible. Sometimes we discuss the events of my week—well, not discuss really. It's more like I listen to my own soliloquy. I try to get Mom to recall memories from her past.

"Do you remember when you spent that year in Chicago?"

She stares at me.

"Remember when you took a vacation to Bermuda?"

A befuddled look spreads across her face.

"Do you ever think about the time you spent in Quebec?"

"No, I don't seem to recall that," she says.

Today I feel sad. My throat is tight, and there are two small tears in the corners of my eyes. Now that I am no longer my mother's primary caregiver in charge of cleaning, feeding, and the rest of her 24/7 regimen, I can just enjoy her.

Not being the master of her little universe has freed me to be Mom's advocate. I closely supervise her care and frequently check in with staff. I actually am comfortable again to spend time with her. Another surprise I discover during our visit.

I inhale deeply. My eyes slowly pan the breakfast table, which now starts to fill with the regular gang. I take in the familiar faces of our Saturday morning crew. Ruby, who usually gives me a happy laugh, is slumped in her wheelchair sleeping. Still wearing her French beret, Freeda is missing more teeth and looks like a Halloween skeleton. Martha, the formerly graceful ballroom dancer, is hunched over at her assigned place, slopping a crooked hand across her plate, desperately trying to get the food into her mouth. But two of our friends are gone now. They have been replaced by two new reasonably lucid recent transfers from "the other side."

"The other side" is the assisted living residence, where the gate is not locked and where the alarm does not sound whenever someone leaves. There people move under their own volition, free and independent to decide where to go and what to do. Free to walk to the park or browse the shops around the corner. To venture anywhere or nowhere in particular.

Freedom and independence are words I remember from my history classes. Now they take on a whole new meaning. A large knot tightens in my stomach to keep my dry throat and watery eyes company. I start to realize that freedom and independence are like time. The less we have of them, the more precious they become.

My gaze rests on my mother. This once spunky and self-sufficient woman now reduced to diapers taught me to iron my shirt, sew a button, cook eggplant parmesan, clean my toilet, and wash my clothes without making them pink. Most important, she taught me how to talk with God.

I remember when my mother taught me to pray. I was four years old. She would lift me into her lap or sit beside me and repeat this prayer:

Dear Little Jesus, teach me good.

Help me do everything I should.

Guide my steps along the way.

So I may be with you someday.

Mom spent this time with me in prayer until I could say these words on my own. Almost sixty years later, I still can remember them.

As I grew older, I became more rebellious. My mother would urge me to pray. The more she insisted, the more intrusive I found both her and God. Eventually, nearly every time, I gave in to her demands.

"Well, if I have to ... I guess" was my standard response between the ages of ten and seventeen. When prayer time rolled around, I learned to shut up and do it with a grunt. I couldn't wait to leave home at eighteen. I lived like many teenagers, in just enough trouble to fit in. I thought of church as just a holiday experience. Then, at nineteen I accepted Jesus Christ. Everything changed. You might think my relationship with my mother would've changed too. But it didn't.

However, I find that now I can appreciate so much. I marvel at this as I hang out with Mom in her lockdown unit. I button her sweater. I feed her some pear on a spoon and remember the good moments. The aroma and savory taste of her home-cooked meals, so faithfully and lovingly prepared. Camping in the backyard and at the state park. Her support during my time with the Cub Scouts and Boy Scouts. Playing canasta and laughing.

I recall her telling me I could do anything if I put my mind to it. She emphasized how important God is. How I could have a relationship with Him, if I wanted it. She had the courage to confront me about certain friends who weren't good for me and to say the truth when it needed to be said. I remember fondly our candlelight Christmas Eve services in the little white church on the New England green. How she encouraged my dad through difficult and challenging times.

Then one day, not too long ago, a clear and powerful thought came to my mind. A thought I would have rejected with vehemence just a few years ago. *I am just like you, Mom.* No, not in the exact warp and woof of life experiences. Not specifically in personality type or temperament. But in the realization that I am a flawed human being, "fearfully and wonderfully made," as Psalm 139 says. That I have strengths and talents that are appreciated. That I am a good person, a fallen person, a complex person in need of Jesus. *Just like you, Mom.*

I wipe the dribble from her chin. She twinkles at me and says, "Thank you, son."

I look into her eyes. "Don't forget, Mom. I love you." *Lord, help me to hold on to the good things and let go when it's time.*

Appendix

Practical Tips

ach of us travels a very personal journey as we care for an aging parent. Even as siblings taking care of the same mom or dad, our individual experiences and need for support can vary widely. It's an emotional roller coaster that can take us to the highest highs, the lowest lows, and through the darkest tunnels.

At various stages of the journey, the physical needs of an aging parent can change rapidly. As we tend to our own children and spouse, job responsibilities, and other obligations, we often don't know how to cope or have time to properly research where to go to obtain the services and support we need to stay balanced and to love our aging parents well. So we include two things we hope will help:

1. **Letters to Mom:** As Dr. Mulder says in his introduction to this book, there's an awful lot of stress on families over things undone. Things that have nothing to

do with the person in the bed. Like guilt—"I wasn't the son I should have been." "I can't let Dad die yet." Writing a letter to a parent can help process those emotions, particularly when an aging parent is not mentally or emotionally capable of dialoging with us. Even when the parent is vibrant, writing a letter helps us gather our wide range of thoughts and feelings. We have included both of our letters for you to read.

2. **Selected Resources:** This is a quick list of solid resources that we think might come in handy as you traverse the unknown road of caring for an aging parent. With the accessibility of information just a computer click away, we do not intend to provide you with a comprehensive list of the nearly unlimited number of resources available. However, in this brief section we have offered a few key national resources that can direct you further to state and local resources for your loved one.

Most importantly, stay encouraged! If our stories have touched you in some way, we'd love to hear from you. Please feel free to contact Ralph at **replumb@aol.com** and Feager at **drfacp@earthlink.net**.

Letters to Mom

An old church hymn says, "On Christ the solid rock I stand all other ground is sinking sand, all other ground is sinking sand!"

Dear Mama,

Thank you for giving us this basic foundation of faith our entire lives. It is because of this foundation that you have three girls "souled out" to Jesus Christ!

I'm so grateful that I can write this letter while you are still here with us. When I reflect on my life, I couldn't have chosen a better mom. Zenobia, Dianne, and I "won" the lottery on you! There is no way that we could have chosen a woman more godly, more compassionate, more generous, more prayerful, more savvy, more encouraging, more supportive, more disciplined, more courageous, more humorous, or more classy than you!

When I reflect upon our childhood, while you were always a little strict, and in my estimation listened to Zenobia a little bit more than you should, what you did always came from a place of love, though at the time it didn't seem like it! We didn't know we weren't rich growing up: every day we had a warm breakfast, a packed lunch, and dinner on the table when we arrived home with dessert; we were always clean from head to toe, with matching socks and ribbons! Who knew you paid two dollars for the dresses and twenty-five cents at Woolworths? We always looked like a million dollars, and so did you!

As we prayed together, which seemed to last hours, went to service, encouraged to be a part of every ministry we were part of (due to Dad being in the military and traveling), having to quote a scripture before we ate dinner, as we sometime rolled our eyes. Who knew then what we know now? You were training us to love and serve God.

How many times did I get popped for rolling my eyes when you said something I didn't like, or swell up like a frog when I was mad at you but dare not say it? I know now what I didn't know then, that discipline brings about great life skills, and it is surely best to be slow to speak, quick to hear, and slow to anger. How many times did you encourage us to do our best and know that there was no one on earth better than the three of us, though you were treated sooooo poorly when you were growing up? I didn't know then what I know now, that when you have great self-esteem, a disciplined prayer life, and the knowledge of how to respect others, there is nothing you can't accomplish as long as you keep God in front.

Your humor and quick wit always hit the nail on the head every single time. This kept us all centered. I can hear your robust laughter that illuminated in the home. We had a great life. I didn't know then what I know now. Laughter is like medicine, as said in the Proverbs.

As we approached adulthood and are now adults, your loving hands of compassion are there, your words of encouragement, your powerful prayers that can kill crickets in the house (LOL), your prayers that can back up a grown man's bowels for messing with one of us (I call them voodoo prayers, LOL), and prayers for many that have been saved, healed, and delivered—God I thank you for my mama! I thank you for a mama who is unashamedly an ambassador for Christ, and so are we. I thank you for a mama who is a clear example of holiness, Your truth, and lives Your word, and now we are too!

So as I see the lights dimming in your eyes, but that brain, that humor, those words of wisdom, those prayers that move mountains remain, I can't even bring myself to think of the day that you won't be with us. So when I cook your meals, help you shower, and wash and lotion your feet; as we take you to the doctor and comfort you, make you laugh, wash your clothes, get everything you need and want, we say we wouldn't have it any other way, because Mama, we do bow down and call you blessed!

I love you with all my heart,
Feager

Dear Louise ... Rita ... Mom,

When I wrote the letter to my dear ten-year-old daughter, Bristol Michelle, the day following her passing into eternity, my heart was full of emotion. Even though it was over twenty-five years ago, I easily remember the words came naturally, with virtually no editing. They were pure and heartfelt, coming from the core of my being. I felt honored when Dr. James Dobson quoted that letter in his book, *When God Doesn't Make Sense.* How I miss you, my angel, born on my birthday, a true gift from God.

Writing this letter is a totally different experience. Memories and emotions are chopped into a cobb salad, jumbled and discordant. Frustration, obligation, guilt, anger, compassion, and unconditional love have each had their season. You are more than likely slumped in your wheelchair in the gate-secured Alzheimer's unit of the senior care facility where you have lived for three years. I see you once per week now, for an hour or so at breakfast time on Saturday mornings. As I sit with my arm around you, playing on my iPhone your favorite hymns—whose words you *still amazingly remember*—I occasionally squeeze your shoulder or massage your neck as we talk ever so occasionally. Then when the food arrives, I help you spoon your cereal one slurp at a time, wipe your mouth with a napkin after you drink your juice, mash the pills into yogurt so you can swallow them, and try to get you to eat some solid food. After I wheel you back to the common area, I pull you out of your chair so we can stretch your back and muscles. You cling to me and say, "I love you, Ralph. Please don't leave me. I'm scared." I assure you that God is always with us and not to be afraid. When I leave the complex the security gate slams behind me. I fight back the tears.

I have tried diligently to piece together the shadows of partial stories from my early childhood, from you and a few reluctant family members before they passed away. I realize that things then, for you and for me, were hard. You were an unwed mother, and I was your bastard child. In those days there was a great deal of shame in such circumstances. But I have come to understand that we all must play that hand that is dealt us. If you get a full house, play it wisely. Some of us don't even get a pair of twos. You, the youngest child of a French Canadian immigrant, herself an orphan, and an alcoholic abusive father created the emotional scars and distrust that framed much of your life. You were misdiagnosed at eighteen and told you would die within a year. You didn't, but something inside you did. Under the circumstances (not all of which are even in this book) you did phenomenally well.

You told me you had to fight hard to keep me. You worked, of course, and I vaguely recall staying with different caregivers. You told me I used to be a happy baby, but that eventually when you came to pick me up after work I would cry and push you away. When, decades later, you told me there were case workers and government agencies involved, I realize it was pretty serious.

From my earliest memory you were an emotional black

hole. A narcissist. Very needy. What narcissist isn't needy? When I was adopted at age five by a loving, simple man, you still clung to me emotionally. That was not a good thing for me. I have jokingly told my closer friends, "It's amazing I'm even half normal" (or at least I'd like to think so). In my fifties I went through an intense period of coming to grips with buried hurt and anger that required much prayer, counseling, and intentional exercises of forgiveness. That's exercises, plural. I made a list of people I needed to forgive, and you were on top of the list. When I read in *Too Soon Old, Too Late Smart* by Gordon Livingston MD that "the statute of limitations has expired on most of our childhood traumas," it made perfect sense to me. Yet it took me years to identify the source(s) of my anger and deal with them. With thanks to God I did so, and made it through.

I am aware that the less we have of something the more valuable it becomes—like air or water or light ... or time. In the context of this life on earth, time is finite and measured. But then as I imagine heaven (as described in John Burke's book by the same name), I am reminded that we have all fallen short; God loves us immeasurably, and He has prepared a place for us where, "He will wipe every tear from their eyes. There will be no more death or mourning or crying or pain, for the old order of things has passed away" (Rev. 21:4 NIV).

When I dealt with my own baggage first and then viewed you—Louise, who hates being called Rita, but loves being called Mom, the way God sees you—my visual acuity changed. It is still true that, "For now we see only a reflection as in a mirror; then face to face. Now I know in part; then I shall know fully, even as I am fully known (I Cor. 13:12 NIV). After all these years, *now* I can see enough to understand. And I understand enough to see!

So, mom, when you cling to me with your head on my chest and say, "I love you," some of it makes sense. Not all of it. Just enough to remind me to trust our sovereign God in all things.

I love you too, Mom …

Even though it took me a few decades to say it from the heart.

Ralph

Resources

In-Home Care and Support

Centers for Medicare and Medicaid Services: www.cms.gov.

Caregiver Resource Kit: www.medicare.gov/campaigns/caregiver/caregiver-resource-kit.html.

Home and Family Caregiving: www.aarp.org/home-family/caregiving/.

Visiting Angels: www.visitingangels.com.

Supplemental assistance with prepared meals: www.mealsonwheelsamerica.org.

Residential Facility-Based Care

A Place for Mom: www.aplaceformom.com.

Residential Care Homes: www.seniorhomes.com.

Housing Help Guide: www.seniorhousingnet.com/care-types/index.aspx.

Senior Daycare

Informed choices for maximum independence: www.resourcesforseniors.com.

Finding the center for your needs: www.helpguide.org.

Mental Health Associations

Alzheimer's Association: www.alz.org.

Government Alzheimer's resources: www.alzheimers.gov.

National Institute on Aging: www.nia.nih.gov.

Support Groups

Family Caregiver Alliance: www.caregiver.org.

A coalition of national organizations focused on family caregiving issues: www.caregiving.org.

National Family Caregivers Association: www.caregiveraction.org.

Financial Resources

Social Security: www.socialsecurity.gov.

State Health Insurance Assistance Program: www.shiptalk.org.

Veterans resources: www.caregiver.va.gov.

Protecting your loved one from elder financial abuse: www.fightback.com.

Senior Advocacy Associations

American Association of Retired Persons: www.aarp.org.

Association of Mature American Citizens: www.amac.org.

American Seniors Association: www.americanseniors.org.

Miscellaneous Resources

Elder Care: www.aging-parents-and-elder-care.com.

A one-stop resource for elder care: www.careforagingparents.com.

Local resources and services: www.eldercare.gov.

The National Clearinghouse for Long-term Care Information: www.longtermcare.gov.

Help finding a caregiver: www.care.com.

Offering elderly clients more than cleaning: www.maids.com.

Essential resources for senior citizens and their caregivers: www.eldercaredirectory.org/state-resources.htm.

Printed in the United States
By Bookmasters